leapfrog
Learners

Oddest Pets

by Annabelle Lynch

First published in 2012 by
Franklin Watts
338 Euston Road
London
NW1 3BH

Franklin Watts Australia
Level 17/207 Kent Street
Sydney
NSW 2000

Copyright © Franklin Watts 2012

Picture credits: Shutterstock: 4br, 4bl, 4tl, 9, 10, 12, 15, 16, 21; rzs/Dreamstime.com: 18; istockphoto: 4tr, 6.

A CIP catalogue record for this book is available from the British Library.

Dewey number: 636'.0887

ISBN 978 1 4451 0323 5 (hbk)
ISBN 978 1 4451 0331 0 (pbk)

Series Editor: Melanie Palmer
Picture Researcher: Diana Morris
Series Advisor: Catherine Glavina
Series Designer: Peter Scoulding

Printed in China

Franklin Watts is a division of Hachette Children's Books,
an Hachette UK company. www.hachette.co.uk

Contents

The words in **bold** can be found in the glossary.

Pick your pet

There are lots of odd pets! Would you like to look after any of these?

You need a lot of time to look after a pet.

Creepy tarantulas

A bee sting hurts more than a tarantula bite!

Tarantulas are big, hairy **spiders**. They look scary, but most can't harm you.

Slithering Snakes

Rock python **snakes** can be kept as pets. They slowly squeeze their **prey** to death, then eat it.

Pythons can live up to 30 years.

Colourful chameleons

Chameleons are **lizards**. They can change the colour of their skin so you can't see them.

Chameleons can move each eye in a different direction.

pot bellied pigs

Most pigs live on farms, but some small pigs can also be good pets. They eat a lot!

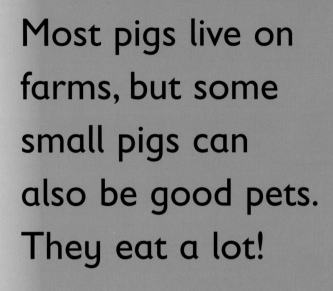

Pot bellied pigs also need plenty of exercise.

Pet insects

A praying mantis is a funny **insect**. Some learn to sit on your hand and take food from it.

Mantis can turn their heads all the way round!

15

Sugar gliders

They feed on sugar and can glide up to **150** metres in the air!

Sugar gliders are **marsupials.** They sleep during the day, but love to play at night.

Nippy pirhanas

Some people keep
fish called piranhas
as pets. They have
very sharp teeth, so
watch your fingers!

Snails are one of the
piranhas favourite foods!

Furless friends

The Chinese crested dog has no **fur**! It smells better than most dogs, but gets cold easily.

Hairless dogs need suncream to protect them.

Glossary

Fur - thick coat of soft hair on an animal

Insect - tiny creature often with many legs

Lizard - long-bodied reptile with legs and tail

Marsupial - animal that has a pouch

Prey - an animal hunted or caught for food

Snake - scaly, legless reptile

Spider - creature with eight legs

Websites:

http://kids.nationalgeographic.com/kids/animals/

http://animal.discovery.com/videos/ top-10-odd-looking-pets/

http://www.petsandkids.co.uk

Quiz

1. What can chameleons do to hide?

2. How do pythons kill their prey?

3. What do pirhana fish have?

4. Which kind of dog has no fur?

5. When do sugar gliders sleep?

6. Which kind of pig makes a good pet?

The answers are on page 24

Answers

1. They change colour
2. They squeeze them to death
3. Sharp teeth!
4. The Chinese crested dog
5. During the day
6. Pot bellied pigs

Index